FOLLOW ME!

FOLLOW ME!

Daily Lent Guide for Families

AMY ROBINSON

kevin
mayhew

For my parents, who gave me a love of stories and seasons:
and with thanks to my husband, who listens to all my stories.

kevin mayhew

First published in Great Britain in 2015 by Kevin Mayhew Ltd
Buxhall, Stowmarket, Suffolk IP14 3BW
Tel: +44 (0) 1449 737978 Fax: +44 (0) 1449 737834
E-mail: info@kevinmayhew.com

www.kevinmayhew.com

9 8 7 6 5 4 3 2 1 0

ISBN 978 1 84867 796 8
Catalogue No. 1501493

Cover design by Rob Mortonson
© Images used under licence from Shutterstock Inc.
Edited by Virginia Rounding
Typeset and illustrations by Melody-Anne Lee

Printed and bound in Great Britain

Contents

About the author

Amy Robinson is a writer, performance storyteller and ventriloquist. As co-founder of Snail Tales she has been telling all sorts of stories in all sorts of places for eight years, and is the benefice children's worker at her own church. She lives in a rectory in Suffolk with the rector, two children and several puppets.

Amy has also written for Kevin Mayhew: *Tales from the Jesse Tree* (1501441), an Advent book of 25 Bible stories, and a DVD and informative handbook: *Performing with Puppets, a Puppeteer's Guide* (1501414). For further details, please see our website: www.kevinmayhew.com

How to use this book

This is a book of stories, activities and reflections for Lent, intended to take a family through the time leading up to Easter.

Each week focuses on one passage from the Bible about being called to follow Jesus. Although the format provides a new activity for every day of the week, the daily suggestions could also be selected and rearranged to provide the basis for a single weekly study or family prayer time, depending on what suits your family best.

For each week, you will find a selection of readings, prayers and activities, all exploring the same story. Readings are taken from the New Revised Standard Version of the Bible, but do use the chapter and verse references to read the story in your family's own preferred version before trying one of the 'retellings'. The 'retellings' present the story using basic storytelling methods, play or poetry to give a different angle or a new point of view. This can be useful for bringing out different questions and for giving you a more direct experience of, and interaction with, the story in the passage. You can read them out loud together, or have a look at them and the tips for telling them, and then put the book down and have a go at storytelling yourselves.

Activities include different ways to retell or play through the story, crafts, suggestions for something to do together as a family, and an invitation to 'go wondering' and think through some questions about the passage. You will also see 'context' sections, which go into more depth by providing some of the surrounding story, relevant passages in other books of the Bible, or historical and cultural information which colours and explains the week's reading.

Since Lent begins on a Wednesday, day five of each week falls on a Sunday and has a 'community activity', which may involve anything from helping a neighbour to asking a friend a question. These suggestions are made with a church meeting in mind, but if you don't attend church they will work just as well in other places: the main thing is to go out and interact with your community.

Be creative with all the suggestions. Depending on the age range of the people who are sharing this book, some activities will work better than others, some will need adapting and some may just not fit. You know your family best. Use what works well, try some new things, come up with ideas of your own and, above all, enjoy exploring together.

The First Disciples

Introduction

In this first story, we look at the moment that Jesus called his very first disciples to follow him. Their calling accompanies a miracle that used their own individual lives and expertise to demonstrate who Jesus was and what he wanted them to do.

Over the course of this week, we will be thinking about how Jesus might call us just as individually. You will discover the reason why Jesus already had such a big crowd following him, put yourselves in the shoes of the fishermen and retell the story with readings, a poem and some fun crafty activities. The community day offers a chance to talk to friends and family and find out how their own journeys of following Jesus began, celebrating each person's individual calling and value to God.

DAY 1

Telling

Once while Jesus was standing beside the lake of Gennesaret, and the crowd was pressing in on him to hear the word of God, he saw two boats there at the shore of the lake; the fishermen had gone out of them and were washing their nets. He got into one of the boats, the one belonging to Simon, and asked him to put out a little way from the shore. Then he sat down and taught the crowds from the boat. When he had finished speaking, he said to Simon, 'Put out into the deep water and let down your nets for a catch.' Simon answered, 'Master, we have worked all night long but have caught nothing. Yet if you say so, I will let down the nets.' When they had done this, they caught so many fish that their nets were beginning to break. So they signalled to their partners in the other boat to come and help them. And they came and filled both boats, so that they began to sink. But when Simon Peter saw it, he fell down at Jesus' knees, saying, 'Go away from me, Lord, for I am a sinful man!' For he and all who were with him were amazed at the catch of fish that they had taken; and so also were James and John, sons of Zebedee, who were partners with Simon. Then Jesus said to Simon, 'Do not be afraid; from now on you will be catching people.' When they had brought their boats to shore, they left everything and followed him.   *Luke 5:1-11*

Retelling

Tips and ideas for telling this story:
The little boat in this story goes through lots of different emotions: worrying that she has done something wrong, feeling surprised when Jesus jumps on board, impressed at Jesus' teaching, proud to be carrying him, afraid when she begins to sink under the weight of the fish, ashamed and embarrassed, happy to have been chosen and called 'useful' by Jesus at the end. Her emotions mirror those of the new disciples to bring life to their experience of being chosen despite feeling unworthy. As you tell the story, put plenty of feeling into the boat's thoughts, trying to use facial expression and tone of voice to convey them. With younger children, you could cut out discs with faces for each emotion and, whenever there is a change, ask the children to choose the one that they think the boat is feeling.

There was once a little fishing boat that lived on the shore of a lake. The lake was so huge that it was known as the Sea of Galilee. Sometimes the waters were still and blue, and at other times there were storms that made the lake as wavy and wild as a real sea. But the fishing boat felt safe there: she knew the lake well, and trusted the fishermen who sailed her.

Every night, the fishing boat sailed out to the middle of the lake, and every night, her fishermen let down nets over her sides and pulled up wriggling, shining fish. Every day at dawn, she carried the fish back to shore. Then the fishermen would take the fresh fish to sell at the market, and spend the rest of the day on the shore, mending and washing their nets and getting ready to go out again when it got dark.

This morning, though, they had not brought back a single fish. Not one! Over and over again, the nets had come up empty. The little boat wondered whether she had done something wrong.

She was distracted from her worries by a loud commotion approaching the shore. A huge crowd of people jostled and elbowed and shouted their way towards her. Just as they reached the place where she was tied up, a man pushed his way out of the crowd and, with a flying leap and a scramble, stood on her deck!

The crowd pressed closer, and the fishing boat worried that they were all going to climb on! But then her fisherman untied her and, joining the strange man on deck, he pushed her away from the shore.

There she floated while the man spoke in a loud voice to all of the people on the shore. And, oh, the things that he said! Such funny stories, such wise and mysterious words, things that were frightening and wonderful and thrilling and strange! The boat felt proud to be a stage for such a fine speaker. She loved everybody looking at her. She wished it could go on for ever.

Eventually, though, the man stopped speaking and turned to the fisherman. 'Let's go further out, and catch some fish,' he said.

The little boat giggled to herself. Whoever heard of catching fish now, in the middle of the day, when they hadn't caught a thing all night! Sure enough, her fisherman was chuckling too. 'We've been out all night and not seen so much as a minnow!' he said. 'Still, you're the boss – let's go!'

The boat floated out towards the middle of the lake, enjoying the wind puffing out her sails, and hoping that the people on the shore were still watching her. Then the fisherman let down the nets, and at once – just like that – they were full! The boat had never felt such a flapping and tugging before. She rocked from side to side, desperately trying to stay upright in the water, as waves splashed over her decks. The fishermen panicked and shouted and pulled. As they lifted the nets, the fish were so heavy that the boat thought she would sink under the weight. The nets began to rip, and the deck filled with flapping tails and shining scales and fishermen slipping and falling on a wriggling tide of wet fish.

In the middle of it all, the strange man sat, quite calm. Suddenly, the boat felt ashamed to be carrying somebody who was obviously so important and powerful. She was embarrassed to think about how, only a moment ago, she had wanted the crowd to admire her. She was only a tiny boat, covered in smelly fish slime, and about to sink and break.

'Go away from me, Lord! I'm a terrible person – I do bad things!' The fisherman was on his knees in all the fish. But the stranger spoke kindly. 'Don't be afraid, Simon. From now on you'll be catching people, with me.' He patted the side of the boat. 'And your little boat here will come in very useful, too,' he smiled.

Once they had got back to the shore and unpacked all the fish, the fishermen followed the man and they disappeared together. They didn't go fishing that night. The little boat wondered whether she would ever carry the strange man who spoke wonderful words again.

She did, in fact, lots of times. But that's another story.

DAY 2

Context

When Jesus called his first disciples, he had to get into a fishing boat because there was such a big crowd waiting to hear him teach. This was very near the beginning of his ministry, so why were so many people already following him? Have a look in your Bible at Luke 4:31-41 first, then read it here in internet click-bait style. Why not make up your own headlines, give a television report or write a newspaper front page to tell these stories along with yesterday's?

This guy was heckling the preacher. You'll never believe what happened next.

In the synagogue on Saturday, a popular new teacher was speaking with amazing authority when a member of the congregation started shouting at him. Witnesses say that he was calling the teacher 'The Holy One of God'.

Benjamin from Capernaum says, 'This guy obviously had something wrong with him. He was yelling at the teacher to go away and leave us alone because he was the Holy One. It sounded like blasphemy to me – he was basically saying that a man was God.'

Strangely, instead of having the heckler escorted from the premises, the teacher, Jesus of Nazareth, started shouting back – but he didn't appear to be talking to the heckler. The truth was altogether weirder.

'He yelled, "Be silent and come out of him!"' says Benjamin, 'and the man just dropped to the floor. But then he got up and he was fine, as sane as you or me. People started saying that Jesus had cast a demon out of him.'

She was sick with a high fever, but then THIS happened.

A woman has an extraordinary story to tell after the new travelling rabbi, Jesus of Nazareth, decided to turn up at her house when she was ill.

'I was really worried because there was no way I could get up and get food and drink for the guests,' she says. 'I couldn't even lift my head from the pillow, I had such a high fever.'

But the unannounced guest walked right into her bedroom, she says. 'He came up to the bed and just told the fever to go away, as if he was talking to a stray dog or something,' she explains. 'And it did! I could get up straight away and get on with everything. I was completely better.'

Crowds of people are waiting outside this house. The reason will surprise you.

Even though it's nearly dark, the huge crowd of people waiting outside this little house is showing no signs of going away. Almost all of them have a disease or a disability – but the man they're waiting for is not a doctor.

'We've heard that Jesus of Nazareth can cure people instantly,' says Joanna, 36, whose daughter has regular fits. 'We're desperate enough to try anything.'

Hannah, 29, breaks through the crowd to show me her son Nathan, a healthy toddler, aged 2. 'He was born with a terrible skin disease that meant he wore bandages all day,' she tells me, 'but look! Jesus touched him and now he's fine!'

As far as anybody knows, this man, Jesus, is a carpenter from Nazareth – but over the past few weeks he has been teaching in the synagogues and his name is connected with several strange incidents and crowds gathering. What will he do next?

DAY 3

Retelling

Tips and ideas for telling this story:
The lines of this poem are very short, but there's a lot packed in. Read it slowly and then read it again – or take it in turns, the second time, reading a verse each. Then have a look at the 'wondering' questions below.

> We were just fishermen
> mending our net,
> then came the day
> we'll never forget.
>
> Huge crowd of people
> filling the beach.
> Man hopped on board,
> started to teach.

After a while
sailing from shore
he asked if we'd like
to catch a few more.

We'd been out all night
caught nothing yet.
But he was in charge.
We let down the net.

No time to question.
No time to think.
Net full, like the beach:
boat starts to sink.

Caught a quick glimpse
of who this must be.
Told him he shouldn't
be dealing with me.

We were just fishermen.
He didn't mind.
Now we'll be fishing
for humankind.

Wondering

Read the poem, and remind yourselves of the Bible reading from Day 1. Then use these questions to 'go wondering' together. Find a quiet moment to read them out loud. Whether you discuss them, try to answer them or simply let them brew in your mind is up to you.

• I wonder what Jesus was saying to the crowds when he talked from the boat?

- I wonder why Simon agreed to cast the net, even though they hadn't caught anything and Jesus wasn't a fisherman?
- I wonder why Simon wanted Jesus to go away from him?
- I wonder what the fishermen thought that 'fishing for people' might mean?
- I wonder what the fishermen left behind to follow Jesus?

DAY 4

Make something

Here are a couple of fun crafts to help you retell the story about Jesus calling the fishermen.

Catch of fish thaumatrope

A thaumatrope is an optical illusion and a toy which was popular among Victorian children. It works by flicking between two pictures so quickly that the brain blends them together into a single image. Thaumatropes are very easy to make and are perfect for illustrating lots of stories.

All you need are two discs of white card (drawing around a roll of sticky tape, or the top of a mug, gives about the right size), some glue, a pencil or straw and something to draw the images with.

On one of the discs, draw lots of fish. On the other disc, draw a grid pattern across the whole circle so that it looks like an empty net.

Glue the discs back to back over the top of the pencil, so that the result looks like a big lollipop with the pencil as the stick and your two drawings on opposite sides.

Now hold the pencil between the palms of your hands, and watch the disc as you rub your hands together. You should see the pictures blend together so that it looks as though the fish are in the net.

Full fishing net

Have a go at making a net full of fish. Several things come in nets – oranges, little cheeses, chocolate coins. Cut fish shapes out of cardboard and wrap them in silver foil, or if you have longer, try sticking on sequins so that they overlap like scales. How many fish can you squeeze into your net?

DAY 5

Community Day

This week's story is all about the first disciples beginning to follow Jesus. Two thousand years later, people still become disciples of Jesus every day. Do you know any of them? For today's community challenge, ask a Christian that you know when and why they started to follow Jesus. You could ask someone at church, or if you don't go to church, you could try a godparent, relative or friend. If you're not sure whether you know any Christians that you could ask, then begin today's community challenge by asking around to find out which of your friends, friends' parents, teachers, local shopkeepers etc., is a Christian – you might be surprised!

(Try to choose people that you already know, and make sure you bring a grown-up with you if you're planning to talk to an unfamiliar person.)

DAY 6

Wondering

Remind yourselves of this week's story if you need to, then 'go wondering' together with these questions. You could try asking them as a meditation by finding a quiet space to sit together. Light some candles or find an object or picture to focus on: you could choose water or floating candles to go with the story. Then choose one person to read the questions clearly, leaving plenty of thinking space between each one. Nobody has to answer out loud.

- Jesus met the fishermen washing their nets. If Jesus came across you doing everyday things, I wonder what you would be doing?

- Jesus got onto Simon's boat to teach the crowds: I wonder how he would use your situation to speak to people?

- Jesus gave Simon a huge catch of fish: I wonder what he would do for you to get your attention?

- Jesus asked Simon to be a fisher of men: I wonder what he would ask you to become?

DAY 7

A Prayer

> Dear Jesus,
> here we are, in our lives,
> surrounded by the things we know well:
> things we are good at, things we like, people we love,
> and things we wish we could change.
> You know it all so well, too.
> Step aboard our lives, Lord Jesus,
> lead us out to risk the deeper water,
> show us what our lives could be with you in charge,
> and use our lives to reveal yourself to others.
> Amen.

The Calling of Levi

Introduction

This week's reading tells the story of the calling of Levi – the disciple also known as Matthew. The call itself is very simple, a blink-and-you'll-miss-it moment, and one can only assume that Jesus' reputation had gone before him for Levi to be so instantly convinced that he wanted to leave everything and respond. The interesting part of the story lies in what happens next. The fact that the ensuing dinner party stirs up grumbling among the Pharisees points out what an extraordinary choice of follower this was, and leads Jesus to make a statement about the kind of person he has come to call. Thankfully, it turns out that Jesus doesn't just call people who think they have their lives sorted out – most of us don't. Instead, he makes a bee-line for broken, messy, imperfect, real people. Jesus says that the healthy don't need a doctor – but are the Pharisees really 'healthy' and not in need of Jesus' help? That will be up to you to decide after you've met a Pharisee on Day 2.

This week, you'll find some readings and retellings to explain who tax collectors and Pharisees were, what they did and why they didn't like each other; some activities which look more closely at Levi's response and at Jesus' metaphorical statement about doctors; and a community day challenge to be welcoming to people who are new or different.

DAY 1

Telling

After this he went out and saw a tax-collector named Levi, sitting at the tax booth; and he said to him, 'Follow me.' And he got up, left everything, and followed him.

Then Levi gave a great banquet for him in his house; and there was a large crowd of tax-collectors and others sitting at the table with them. The Pharisees and their scribes were complaining to his disciples, saying, 'Why do you eat and drink with tax-collectors and sinners?' Jesus answered, 'Those who are well have no need of a physician, but those who are sick; I have come to call not the righteous but sinners to repentance.'

Luke 5:27-32

Retelling

Tips and ideas for telling this story:
Why not write this short letter from Levi into an invitation card and take it out of an envelope to read it? As you read, imagine being Levi's friends. Are you surprised by his invitation? Will you go to the dinner? What do you think it will be like?

Dear friends,

You are invited to a feast at my house, tomorrow, starting at midday. Please come and bring all your friends, especially the ones who collect taxes in other areas and villages. No expense will be spared.

The guest of honour is an extraordinary man called Jesus, who has changed my life. Today he walked past the office where I was sitting, taking taxes (and, as my usual practice has been, asking for extra money to keep for myself before paying the Romans). It was a fleeting moment: I almost missed it. He barely stopped walking, just turned as he passed and looked me in the eye. 'Follow me,' he said, and kept on going. It was a split-second decision: the easiest, hardest and best decision I have ever made.

At tomorrow's dinner, I will also be announcing my immediate retirement from the tax-collecting business. Perhaps somebody could clear my desk. I won't be in tomorrow.

All my best wishes,

Levi

DAY 2

Context

Hello, my name is Phineas, and I'm a Pharisee. Pleased to meet you. Come on, shake my hand, I won't bite! We Pharisees get a bad rap in the Gospels, but really we're just the same as your religious teachers and leaders today – we spend our time working out what God's word is, and then making sure that everyone is following it. Anyway, I'm happy to answer any questions you have.

What's wrong with tax collectors, you say? Don't you have them in your country? They take money from us Jews, on behalf of the Romans, and give it to them, our oppressors. Anyone who accepts that kind of job from the enemy is a traitor. And most of them ask for even more than they've been told to collect, and then pocket the extra. Greedy, lying, scrounging scoundrels, the lot of them.

What do you mean, what if they can't get any other job? They just have to work harder, like us. Plenty of jobs going.

The others at Levi's dinner? They were all a bad lot. None of them the kind of person a decent teacher of the law would associate with. Yes, I know nobody's perfect, but these people weren't just ordinary citizens who get things wrong now and then. They were persistent breakers of the law. People who make a living by getting things wrong. People who base their entire existence, lifestyle, identity on breaking the law. Being nice to them isn't going to change anything.

Oh, I know Jesus was very clever with his 'only sick people need a doctor' line, but these aren't just sick people – they're terminal. Best leave them to get on with it.

At least he acknowledges that we're the healthy ones. Not so sure about him, though. That doctor ought to cure himself, if you ask me.

No more questions? Well, it was good to meet you. See you in the synagogue on Saturday? No? Well, suit yourself . . .

Think about it . . .

Are there any equivalents of tax collectors in our society today? Who are they, and why are they unpopular? Is there any such thing as a 'hopeless case'? How can Christians best live out Jesus' attitude to these people?

And are the Pharisees really 'the healthy ones', or has Phineas the Pharisee misunderstood what Jesus was saying?

DAY 3

Context

In between calling the fishermen and calling Levi, Jesus encountered two people and healed them. Have a look at their stories.

> Once, when he was in one of the cities, there was a man covered with leprosy. When he saw Jesus, he bowed with his face to the ground and begged him, 'Lord, if you choose, you can make me clean.' Then Jesus stretched out his hand, touched him, and said, 'I do choose. Be made clean.' Immediately the leprosy left him. And he ordered him to tell no one. 'Go,' he said, 'and show yourself to the priest, and, as Moses commanded, make an offering for your cleansing, for a testimony to them.' But now more than ever the word about Jesus spread abroad; many crowds would gather to hear him and to be cured of their diseases.
>
> *Luke 5:12-15*

One day, while he was teaching, Pharisees and teachers of the law were sitting near by (they had come from every village of Galilee and Judea and from Jerusalem); and the power of the Lord was with him to heal. Just then some men came, carrying a paralysed man on a bed. They were trying to bring him in and lay him before Jesus; but finding no way to bring him in because of the crowd, they went up on the roof and let him down with his bed through the tiles into the middle of the crowd in front of Jesus. When he saw their faith, he said, 'Friend, your sins are forgiven you.' Then the scribes and the Pharisees began to question, 'Who is this who is speaking blasphemies? Who can forgive sins but God alone?' When Jesus perceived their questionings, he answered them, 'Why do you raise such questions in your hearts? Which is easier, to say, "Your sins are forgiven you," or to say, "Stand up and walk"? But so that you may know that the Son of Man has authority on earth to forgive sins' – he said to the one who was paralysed – 'I say to you, stand up and take your bed and go to your home.' Immediately he stood up before them, took what he had been lying on, and went to his home, glorifying God. Amazement seized all of them, and they glorified God and were filled with awe, saying, 'We have seen strange things today.'

Luke 5:17-26

Both these men had physical ailments, and Jesus healed both of them – but something else happened in these encounters as well. Jesus told the man with leprosy not to tell anyone, but to prove that he was really well by going to the temple and making the offerings that were commanded for someone who had been cured of that disease. His actions would demonstrate his faith, gratitude and the miracle that had taken place without the need for him to put it into words. Later, Jesus told the paralysed man that his sins were forgiven, before anything about healing was mentioned.

Only sick people need a doctor – and both of these people were sick and did need healing – but Jesus saw that each of them needed something else even more: a restored relationship with God.

DAY 4

Act

Levi's first response after following Jesus is to invite all his friends for a banquet to meet Jesus. As a family, think of someone you could invite for tea, a meal or to come to church with you tomorrow.

DAY 5

Community Day

The first disciples accepted this new follower of Jesus, who came from a completely different background and wasn't very popular. They went for a meal at his house as his guests and friends, even though that led to the Pharisees asking them difficult questions about what Jesus was up to!

Do you know anyone who is new to your school, church, work or community? What could you do to welcome and accept them? As a family, think of a few welcoming ideas and make a note to do them in your diary. Today, why not write them a card to say that you've enjoyed meeting them and hope they are settling in. Or, just go and tell them!

DAY 6

Play

Here is a short, silly sketch based on Jesus' metaphor about who needs a doctor. You could dress up to act it out yourselves, make paper puppets to be the characters, or play it through using dolls or teddies. Perhaps you can think of an audience and prepare a performance?

The scene is the outside of a hospital. Doctors are gathered around, wearing white coats. An enthusiastic junior doctor arrives. The conversation is between the junior doctor and the other doctors: you could play it with only two people, one saying all the lines marked 'Doctors', or you could have several doctors and split those lines up between them.

Junior: Here I am! I've made it! Wow, it's great to be here! Is this the way in?

Doctors: Hold on! You don't want to go in there!

Junior: Isn't this the hospital?

Doctors: Yes, of course it is!

Junior: Well, then – why shouldn't I go in?

Doctors: There are sick people in there! You might catch something!

Junior: Oh, no, that's all right. You see (*proudly*), I'm a doctor.

Doctors: We're doctors too, but that doesn't make us immune to diseases.

Junior: Wait a minute. You're doctors too? Well then – what are you doing out here?

Doctors: You're new, aren't you?

Junior: Yes! Newly qualified. I've just passed all my exams. I can't wait to start treating real patients!

Doctors: Well, newbie, you have a lot to learn.

Junior: I do?

Doctors: Yes! Sick people are dangerous! They have germs. Some of them are really messy. Sometimes, they're (*shudders*) bleeding!

Junior: But . . . isn't that the point of being a doctor? Learning how to make them better?

Doctors:	Ahhh, listen to you! So young and naïve. I remember being young, like you. When I was young I thought I could solve the world's problems, too, but that's just not the way things are.
Junior:	(*peering through the windows*) Look, the people in there really need our help! That girl looks as if she's broken her arm . . .
Doctors:	(*without moving, yawns*) Yes, we get that a lot. She should have been more careful.
Junior:	And I think that one's having a heart attack!
Doctors:	Ah, well. Heart attacks are usually fatal.
Junior:	Exactly! So . . . shouldn't we go in, and help?
Doctors:	How can you tell that they want us to help? They might think we're interfering!
Junior:	But they can't look after themselves! We have to go in, come on!
Doctors:	Oooh, no. I wouldn't want to get involved with that. Probably nothing we can do at this stage, anyway. Best just leave them to it.
Junior:	But didn't you go to medical school to learn how to . . . Oh, forget it. This is ridiculous. I'm going in! (*runs into the hospital*)
Doctors:	(*after a moment, looking through the window*) Dear me, these idealist youngsters and their funny newfangled ideas. Sick people need our help? Whatever next? . . .

All freeze, and a narrator/voiceover says:
Jesus said: 'Healthy people don't need a doctor – sick people do. I didn't come to call perfect people, but to help people who get things wrong to turn back to God.'

DAY 7

Prayer Activity

You will need: a packet of sticking plasters, paper, pens and a quiet place. You might like to draw or print the outline of a body on each person's piece of paper.

Remind everyone of Jesus' saying: 'Healthy people don't need a doctor, but sick people do.' Jesus was saying that when people turn away from God and get things wrong, they can be like sick people who need help from a doctor to get better.

Sit quietly for a moment, or listen to some quiet music. Then read the passage about the calling of Levi again. Ask each person to think silently of things they would like forgiveness for, and as they think of them, to make marks on their paper, showing that these are things that will need help to get better. Read this prayer out loud:

> Jesus,
> you said that you didn't come to help perfect people.
> You came to help people who get things wrong.
> Nobody is perfect,
> and we all get things wrong.
> We can all think of things we shouldn't have done,
> or things that we should have done, but didn't.
> Thank you for coming to help us.
> We're sorry when we hurt you, other people and ourselves.
> Please heal and forgive us.

Next, let everyone stick on the plasters to cover all of the marks that they made. Just as doctors use their skill with medicines or bandages to heal people, Jesus is able to take away the guilt for things we do wrong because of his death for us on the cross.

Counting the Cost

Introduction

This week, we'll be looking at the costs of our life choices as we try to understand what Jesus meant when he advised his potential followers to count the cost of becoming his disciples. In this passage, Jesus says that the cost is high: he mentions carrying a cross, and being ready to give up all your possessions. It's a serious warning, but perhaps not one meant to put off true disciples. In two mini-parables, Jesus points out the wisdom of estimating the cost of anything worth doing if you are serious about succeeding: this week's retelling explores the consequences both of choosing for, and choosing against the costly option. Later in the week, we will see that another of Jesus' parables shows just how much the kingdom of heaven is really worth, and we will investigate what the cost of following Jesus looks like in our lives as well as in different parts of the world today.

DAY 1

Telling

Whoever does not carry the cross and follow me cannot be my disciple. For which of you, intending to build a tower, does not first sit down and estimate the cost, to see whether he has enough to complete it? Otherwise, when he has laid a foundation and is not able to finish, all who see it will begin to ridicule him, saying, 'This fellow began to build and was not able to finish.' Or what king, going out to wage war against another king, will not sit down first and consider whether he is able with ten thousand to oppose the one who comes against him with twenty thousand? If he cannot, then, while the other is still far away, he sends a delegation and asks for the terms of peace. So therefore, none of you can become my disciple if you do not give up all your possessions.

Luke 14:27-33

Retelling

Tips and ideas for telling this story:

When Jesus talked about estimating the cost of building a tower, what kind of tower might he have meant? The Bible is full of references to watchtowers, which were built in vineyards to protect the harvest from thieves and to shelter the workers there from the midday sun, prowling wild animals and every danger in between. It seems likely that the image of a tower in the minds of Jesus' listeners would have been one of these watchtowers. You could use the internet to find an image of a vineyard and watchtower before telling the story.

Throughout the Bible, the presence of the watchtower in the vineyard is compared to the presence of God in a person's life. (Look, for example, at Proverbs 18:10 and 2 Samuel 22:3.) So why is a vineyard without a watchtower like a life without God? What problems and motives might make us similar to a person who has run out of resources and failed to complete the watchtower? And what might be the consequence of not counting the cost properly and leaving the tower unfinished? Expanding Jesus' metaphor into a story gives us a chance to explore these questions and to find a deeper understanding of what Jesus was saying.

Watchtowers and vineyards were the property and concern of the whole family, and since this is a story about a family, yours can join in with all the actions involved in planting a vineyard as you tell the story.

Once, there was a family who decided to plant a vineyard. Dad, Mum and children all agreed to help. Grandma and Grandpa agreed to help.

Even Great-Grandma, though she couldn't do much exercise any more, agreed to help by drawing out plans and ordering everybody else about!

First, they had to clear the ground by picking up all the stones that might get in the way. (Go on, everybody, pick up those stones!)

Next, they had to build a fence around the edge of the land, so that everyone would know it was theirs. (Can you all hold hands, arms stretched out, to be a fence?)

Then, they had to plough the land and break up the soil ready for planting. (Can you all pretend to dig, or push a plough back and forth?)

Finally, they had to plant their seeds and water them. (Can you pretend to plant seeds in rows, counting them as you go?)

At last, they all sat down . . . and worried.

'How will we know when the grapes are ready?' asked one of the children.

'What if someone else comes and picks them when we're not looking?' asked Mum.

'What if birds and animals dig up the seeds before they grow?' worried Dad.

'What if a bear comes while we're working out here?' asked the littlest child.

Everybody looked at Great-Grandma. She was very wise.

'You need a watchtower,' she explained, 'a tall, strong tower. You can look out at the vines from the top and see which grapes are ready. You can watch for animals and other people picking them. And if a wild animal comes, you can hide inside the tower. When you bring the harvest in, you can keep the grapes in the tower so that nobody can steal them, and before that you can store all your tools in the tower, safe from thieves. When the children are working and playing among the vines, Mum and Dad will be able to watch from the tower and see that they are all safe, and call out to them if they see danger. And when you need a place to rest and eat lunch when the sun is hottest, you can come and rest in the shade inside. You need a watchtower!'

Everybody agreed, and got straight to work. Dad fetched stone. Grandma and Grandpa drew designs. The children dug foundations. Soon, the tower was a short round wall, just as high as the littlest child's head.

At that point, Dad looked very worried. 'There's no stone left,' he said. 'We won't be able to finish our tower.'

'Fetch some more!' said the children.

'There's no money left to pay for more,' said Mum.

'I wanted a smart tower in our vineyard to do all those things that Great-Grandma told us about,' said Dad, sadly. 'I didn't think to work out how much it was going to cost to build one.'

'We'll have to wait until our first harvest,' said Grandpa, 'and use the money we get from the grapes to complete the tower.'

'But without a tower,' Great-Grandma pointed out, 'there might not be a good harvest. We should have spent less on the fence, or bought less land, or planted fewer seeds. The watchtower is the most important part of looking after a vineyard, but we left it until last.'

I wonder what the family can do? Why not write an ending to their story? Is there a way that it could still end positively? (Clue: look at the parable on Day 3 of this week and see whether it contains a solution to the family's problem!)

Or, you could have a go at creating your own story from the other metaphor that Jesus used – about a king who goes to war without working out whether he has enough soldiers. What happens to him? Is there a way for the story to end peacefully?

DAY 2

Context

'Salt is good; but if salt has lost its taste, how can its saltiness be restored? It is fit neither for the soil nor for the manure heap; they throw it away. Let anyone with ears to hear listen!' (Luke 14:34-35).

Jesus says this about salt, in Luke's account, straight after talking about counting the cost. You can find a similar passage in Matthew 5:13-16, where Jesus says that his disciples are the salt of the earth and the light of the world. Why might Luke have mentioned it here? It seems odd and out of context, yet in some translations it is even linked with a word like 'therefore'.

The basic property of salt is to be salty. That's what it does! Apart from being 'white' and 'a crystal', it can really only be described by the way that it tastes. If it no longer tasted of salt, it would literally be good for nothing.

Perhaps Jesus is implying that, as salt is defined by tasting salty, discipleship is defined by following him as an absolute priority. Speaking to this crowd of people who have been tagging along without committing or changing their lives, he points out a gap between what they say they want, and whether it shows in what they do. They need to discover what the cost of discipleship is – not in order to pay it, but to see what they would already have done if they had really been listening. The way to test salt is to taste it, and the way to test a true disciple is to see that Jesus comes first in their lives.

Today, here are some things you could do to help you think about salt:

- Have a taste test with some salt 'n' shake crisps, the kind that come with a little blue sachet of salt to add. Add no salt to one packet, half the salt to another, and all the salt to a third. Take it in turns to wear a blindfold and sample them. Can you taste the difference? Can you tell which one has the most and least salt?

- Make some salt dough. It's very easy: use a small glass or cup as your basic measure and use one of salt, two of flour and one of water (mix the water in gradually to get the perfect consistency). Use the dough to make a model of something of yours that is very precious to you. Talk about your models and why you've chosen those particular things, and thank God for giving them to you. Explain that good things are gifts from God, and that's why he is still more important than any of them!

DAY 3

Context

In Matthew's Gospel, Jesus compares finding the kingdom of heaven to finding priceless treasure, or a very expensive pearl – worth giving up everything to claim it. When Jesus mentions being ready to give up all your possessions in this week's main reading, it sounds challenging and scary, and so it should – Jesus meant to challenge the crowd around him. However, when we look at the command to give everything up in the light of this parable, we begin to see that this sacrifice naturally pours out from the joy of discovering the riches, value and eternal life of the kingdom that Jesus offers in exchange.

> 'The kingdom of heaven is like treasure hidden in a field, which someone found and hid; then in his joy he goes and sells all that he has and buys that field.'

> 'Again, the kingdom of heaven is like a merchant in search of fine pearls; on finding one pearl of great value, he went and sold all that he had and bought it.'
>
> *Matthew 13:44-46*

Here is a way to tell the parable of the pearl. It's a bit like a memory game, and it's lots of fun. Get everyone involved – the more suggestions to remember, the more fun it is!

Once upon a time, there was a very rich merchant. He was so rich that he owned a huge house, and inside his house he put everything he'd ever wanted because he was rich enough to buy it all! (Ask the children to say what they think the merchant had in his house, or what they would put in a house if they could buy anything they wanted. Accept all answers – when I've done this story in schools, the merchant has owned everything from iPads to a solid gold toilet! Try to remember each of the suggestions, creating an action and a sound for each one to help you all remember.

With my two examples, you might pretend to hold an iPad and tap the screen saying 'Tap, tap', then pretend to flush the toilet and make a flushing sound.) Sometimes, the merchant would just sit in his house and look at it all, feeling very happy.

One day, the merchant went for a walk and he happened to pass a jewellery shop. In the window was a magnificent pearl. One look at the pearl told the merchant that it must be worth much more than his . . . (go through the list again, with all the actions and sounds, trying to remember everything in order). And he wanted it!

So the merchant went into the shop and asked how much the pearl was, but when he heard the price, he was very sad. The jeweller wanted more than the cost of his . . . (go through the list again, a bit faster this time!) all put together!

The merchant went home to his big house. But as he sat and looked at his (list again, even faster), he only felt more miserable. Suddenly, he realised that he wanted that pearl more than any of those things!

The merchant got up and started to put all his stuff into a shopping trolley. He put in his . . . (go through the list again, faster, enjoying the absurdity that comes with imagining how to fit racing cars and swimming pools into a shopping trolley!). He pushed it all to market, calling out, 'Who wants to buy my . . . ?' (list again, very fast!).

Once he had sold it all, he still didn't have enough, so he went back home and put up a 'for sale' sign on his front lawn. Before long, the big, empty house was sold. Then the merchant raced back to the jewellery shop, and with every last penny of the money he'd got from selling everything, he bought the pearl. He sat and looked at it, and he was very happy.

Jesus said that finding the kingdom of heaven is like finding that pearl. Suddenly you know that you have come across the most precious and valuable thing in the world, and you would give up anything to have it.

DAY 4

Activity

Today's activity is all about counting and comparing the costs of living. Here are some things you could try:

- If you go shopping or go out today, note down how much each of you spends and add it all up to see how much today cost the whole family. Was it worth it?

- Make a note of everything you consume today: bus fares and petrol, toilet paper and food, cleaning products, heating, electricity, even television! See if you can estimate the cost of a day's life.

- Choose some everyday things for the children to find out the cost: for example, favourite sweets, swimming lessons, a week's groceries. Find out what it costs you to be able to eat, or to do your favourite hobby. Then think outside of money: what does it cost, for example, in time spent shopping or getting to your activity? What does it cost in terms of other things you could be doing, or things your friends get up to while you are enjoying your hobby? Is it still worth it? Why?

- What costs your family the most in money and time? Is it the thing that is most worth having or doing?

Here are some estimated costs to start you off:

Pets: The average lifetime cost of owning a dog today stands at around £16,900 and for a cat £17,200, according to research by a pet insurance company: and it's set to get even more expensive. The average annual cost of owning a dog is currently £1183. A horse costs about £1800 a year, a hundred times more expensive than a hamster at £18 a year.

Children: The average cost of raising a child in England is £230,000. Parents who use disposable nappies can expect to spend about £800 on nappies alone in the first two years of a child's life – that's an estimated 5353 nappies! In 2013, a report found that the average cost of kitting a child out with school uniform was £156 for primary and £285 for secondary school, while research by a major supermarket chain found families spending £312 per child on Christmas presents – which seems more reasonable when you consider that the average child's Christmas wishlist added up to £900!

Household: A recent report on family spending from the Office for National Statistics shows that, for two parents and two children in England, the average weekly spend on food and non-alcoholic drinks is £83.60. Include alcohol and tobacco and the cost goes up to £96. The average household energy bill for a year was £1,352 in 2013, according to an online price comparison company. The average cost of running a car in 2015 is £3500 per year.

DAY 5

Community Day

Count the cost, in time, money and resources, of doing something as a family to help somebody else in the next few days. Could you invite someone for a meal, donate to a foodbank, or give some of your things away to a charity shop? Perhaps you could give your time to be sponsored, doing something to raise money for charity?

Try Oxfam Unwrapped for some ideas that are easy to count. Did you know that £25 could buy a goat, or £8 could buy school supplies for a child in a Third World country? For a more ongoing difference, you could consider sponsoring a child: the cost to your family is about £25 a month, depending on the sponsorship programme that you choose, as well as your time in writing letters and praying for your sponsored child. Child sponsorship can radically change the lives of children in some of the world's poorest countries.

Whatever you choose, once you have counted the cost and decided that it's something worth doing, try persuading another person that it's worth doing, too!

Or this: today is Mothering Sunday. Count up all the things that your mother does and has done for you – and then find a way to say a huge thank you!

DAY 6

There are some places in the world where the cost of following Jesus is very high. Spend some time today finding out about one of those places, and praying for the followers of Jesus who live there. Perhaps you know of a place in the news at the moment; otherwise, here are some real people and situations to start off your investigation.

- Meriam Ibrahim, the woman who was imprisoned and threatened with death in Sudan after marrying a Christian. She refused to renounce her faith, and gave birth to her daughter in prison.

- The persecution of Christians in Iraq and Syria by ISIS: in 2014 the city of Mosul was emptied of Christians for the first time in 1600 years when they were told to convert to Islam, leave or die.

- The rapid growth of Christianity in China has led to the destruction of even the official, government-approved churches – while meeting in a house church is illegal. In April 2014, thousands of Chinese Christians surrounded a church in Wenzhou, known as 'the Jerusalem of the East', to stop officials from bulldozing it to the ground.

- In February 2015, 21 Coptic Christians were beheaded in Libya by Islamic State.

- In March 2015, the Pope said that the world was trying to hide persecution against Christians, after terrorists bombed two churches in Pakistan.

A prayer

Lord Jesus, there are some places in our world where the cost of following you is very high. Today we are sad as we think about our Christian brothers and sisters in . . . (name the place you have investigated, and tell Jesus about some of the things that are happening there).

Jesus, we thank you for the faith and example of these people, and we pray that they know you are there with them, giving them strength to face the dangers, and hope of eternal life with you. We pray for your peaceful kingdom to come. Amen.

If you have found out about several places, you could pray with a world map spread out on the floor. Help the children to find each place on the map, and put a lit tealight (the electric ones are safer) over the places, as you pray for the light of Christ to shine on the situation and the people there.

DAY 7

Wondering

Think back over this week's activities and ask everybody: what did you enjoy doing together this week? What made you think? Have you found out anything new? What sticks in your mind the most from the readings and activities this week?

Read the very first reading from Day 1 again, and then 'go wondering' together. You could light some candles and play quiet music in the background. Choose one person to read the questions, leaving space for thinking time in between each one: nobody has to answer out loud.

• I wonder why Jesus wanted people to know that following him could be hard?

- I wonder whether anybody listening to Jesus decided to stop following him when they heard him talking about the cost?
- I wonder whether anybody decided to follow him more closely?
- I wonder whether following Jesus feels costly or difficult for me?
- I wonder whether I would still follow Jesus if it became really difficult?
- I wonder what Jesus would say to me about following him?

The Rich Young Ruler

Introduction

After looking into Jesus' saying about counting the cost, this week we meet a man who felt unable to follow Jesus when he knew what the cost was going to be. In contrast to the disciples we've come across so far, this person's response to a direct invitation from Jesus was to turn away sadly. Jesus responds by telling his disciples that it is harder for a rich person to enter the kingdom of heaven than it is for a camel to squeeze through the eye of a needle, but he also has comforting words when his disciples are understandably disheartened by this piece of information! Through readings and activities this week, we will investigate the attitude of the rich young ruler, meet a camel and a monkey, find ways to practise generosity and thank God that, with him, nothing is impossible.

DAY 1

Telling

A certain ruler asked him, 'Good Teacher, what must I do to inherit eternal life?' Jesus said to him, 'Why do you call me good? No one is good but God alone. You know the commandments: "You shall not commit adultery; You shall not murder; You shall not steal; You shall not bear false witness; Honour your father and mother."' He replied, 'I have kept all these since my youth.' When Jesus heard this, he said to him, 'There is still one thing lacking. Sell all that you own and distribute the money to the poor, and you will have treasure in heaven; then come, follow me.' But when he heard this, he became sad; for he was very rich. Jesus looked at him and said, 'How hard it is for those who have wealth to enter the kingdom of God! Indeed, it is easier for a camel to go through the eye of a needle than for someone who is rich to enter the kingdom of God.'

Those who heard it said, 'Then who can be saved?' He replied, 'What is impossible for mortals is possible for God.'

Luke 18:18-27

Retelling

Tips and ideas for telling this story:
This retelling paints the rich young ruler in a certain light, and of course there are many possible motives and backgrounds that can be imagined for him – this is only a guess at one. Narrating the story through the camel's eyes is an interesting way of exploring the themes of wealth literally weighing someone down, and of the need to follow a master. In Matthew 6:24, Jesus says that nobody can follow two masters: it's either God or money.

Feel free to use a grumpy camel voice to tell this story, or even to use a puppet or soft toy camel to whisper into your ear while you 'translate'! But don't make the camel's character too one-dimensional, because he has important things to say, and a really silly voice would distract from the sad ending.

My master's always been able to get his own way, and I should know. He's been ordering me about for years, and I've never seen him fail to get exactly what he wants. You name it, he owns it: and if he didn't inherit it from his millionaire dad, he buys it for himself – and then it's me that has to carry it. He has five camels, and I'm his favourite. I think it's because I'm the biggest. He can fit more on me. You wouldn't believe what he takes with him, even just for a short trip into town: clothes and carpets and cushions, boxes and bangles and bling.

It's all for show, you see. If he spots anything he fancies, whatever it is and whoever it belongs to, he just sidles up to the owner with me in tow and says, 'Now, my good man, what would I have to do to acquire that fine jar of perfume?' They take one look at him flashing his rings and his robes, and they're so impressed that they sell it to him half-price in the hope he'll become a regular customer. He's very slick – or he was, until today.

Today, he wasn't getting all the attention he's used to. The adoring crowds weren't gawping at us: they were listening to this teacher telling stories. As we approached, the teacher was saying something about entering the kingdom of heaven, and he was pointing at a child as he said it. I could tell my master was interested. Sure enough, when the teacher finished speaking, he sidled up to him.

'Good teacher, what must I do to inherit eternal life?' As if he hadn't inherited enough already. If camels could blush, I would have been scarlet.

The teacher looked at him, and I got the impression that the flashy rings and robes weren't doing their usual job.

'Only God can be called "good",' he said. 'Don't you know the commandments? No adultery, no murder, no stealing, no lying, honour your father and mother?'

'I've been obeying all those since I was that size,' replied my master, pointing to the little child that the teacher had been talking about before.

The teacher looked from my master to the wide-eyed child and back again, and he suddenly looked terribly sad. 'You're missing something,' he said. 'Sell everything you have, and give your money to the poor. Then you will have treasure in heaven. And then, come and follow me.' He held out his hand.

I don't know how my master resisted following him. If camels had hands, I would have given him mine. I think my master nearly did. For a moment, he relaxed his grasp on my leading rope, but then he grabbed it back again. Looking down at the floor, he turned to walk away and tugged on the rope.

Camels can be stubborn, but I wasn't being stubborn – I just wasn't ready to move. Something odd had happened and I wasn't sure what it was, and I wanted to stay near the teacher. I somehow didn't fancy going back to my palatial stable and wearing my shiny gold harness. The rope tugged, but I stood still, and for a moment the teacher and I looked into each other's eyes. Then he put his hand on my nose.

'It's very hard for a rich person to enter the kingdom of heaven,' he said, softly. 'It would be easier for a camel to fit through the eye of a needle.'

I thought that was a bit unnecessary, if I'm honest. It wasn't my fault that I was covered in bags and boxes and enough gold to sink a small armada. One of the teacher's friends threw both hands in the air in a gesture of frustration. 'Who can be saved, then?!' he asked. Good question. The teacher smiled.

'What is impossible for people is possible with God,' he said. My master gave another hard tug on my rope. The teacher nodded, and patted my neck, and my master led me away.

DAY 2

Context

An ancient fable exists in both India and Africa about how to trap a monkey. It is only very short, and appears in many forms including story, fable, idiom and riddle. Here is my version, in rhyme:

> A traveller in a land afar
> carried snacks inside a jar.
> Beneath a tree the traveller slept,
> and to his side a monkey crept.
> In the jar some nuts he spied
> and quickly stuck his hand inside.
> The jar was narrow as his wrist,
> so, with the nuts clenched in his fist,

he couldn't pull his hand back through.
He couldn't work out what to do.
Without the nuts he wouldn't go,
but, with the nuts, he couldn't: so . . .
I don't know – can you tell me?
Was he trapped, or was he free?

- What do you think the answer is?
- What does the monkey need to do to be free?
- Do you think there are any similarities between the monkey with his fist trapped in the jar and the rich young ruler?

Some people think that Jesus was using a very similar image to the monkey jar when he talked about putting a camel through the eye of a needle. The theory goes that the Needle's Eye was the name of a very narrow gate in Jerusalem, at which merchants would have to unload their camels in order to fit them through, leaving all their merchandise on the other side. Do you think that sounds likely, or was Jesus just intending it to be an image of complete impossibility?

DAY 3

Craft

'Sell all that you own and distribute the money to the poor, and you will have treasure in heaven' (Luke 18:22).

Make a treasure-in-heaven box by reusing any small cardboard box, or by folding a cube out of paper. You could give your box a curved top and decorate it like a treasure chest. Next, cut out small rectangles of coloured paper and decorate them to look like bank notes, but leave a space somewhere on them to write.

When you see a member of the family putting someone else before themselves or giving generously, write their name and the deed on a note and put it in the box. Everybody can join in with this – if you can't write yet, then draw a picture or ask someone else to help you! Look out for each other, and try hard to catch generous actions like offers of help, sharing of toys and giving of time.

You could also think of generous family activities that would fill the box up faster: giving toys and clothes away to charity, for example, or volunteering your time to go to an event or help a neighbour.

When the box is full (or when you've used up all the notes), get together and read some of the generous things that you've done for each other and for other people. Choose a family treat, like an outing, to do together as a celebration.

DAY 4

Context

In this week's reading, Jesus reminded the rich young ruler of some of the ten commandments. Do you know what they are? Before you look at the list below, see how many you can remember – or guess – and write them down to compare!

How many did you get right? Here are the ten commandments that God gave to Moses for his people to follow. You can find them in your Bible in Exodus 20:1-17.

1. There is only one God.
2. Do not worship idols.
3. Respect the name of God.
4. Keep the Sabbath holy as a day of rest.
5. Honour your father and mother.
6. Do not murder.
7. Do not commit adultery.
8. Do not steal.
9. Do not lie.
10. Do not covet anything that somebody else owns.

Have a look back at the reading for this week. Which of the commandments does Jesus mention to the rich young ruler? Which ones doesn't he mention?

The rich young ruler says that he has followed all the commandments since he was a child, but I wonder whether he is really following the ones that Jesus leaves out. Is it possible to be rich without coveting things that other people have? In today's materialistic society, the pattern seems to be that the more you own, the more you want.

What about the other commandments that Jesus leaves out? When he is talking to the rich young ruler, he lists the commandments that have to do with other people, but he doesn't mention commandments 1 to 4: the ones that talk about our relationship with God. Do you think the rich young ruler is following those as well? Why, or why not? How might Jesus' request to the rich young ruler – to leave everything and follow him – make a difference to how he keeps those first commandments?

DAY 5

Community Day

A generous act: make or buy cakes or biscuits to share after church today; or, if you don't go to church, think of a neighbour, old people's home or staff common room that would appreciate them. If you made a treasure-in-heaven box on Day 3 this week, this counts as one note to put into it!

DAY 6

Prayer

'What is impossible for mortals is possible for God' (Luke 18:27). Although it ought to be impossible for us to enter the kingdom of God, Jesus died to make it possible. Today, here are some ideas for grateful prayers. You could choose one, two or a few, or combine them to make them suitable for your family's age groups; or you could each choose one to do separately.

- **Listen to some thankful music.** Try *Amazing Grace, When I Survey the Wondrous Cross, Once Again* by Matt Redman or *How He Loves* by John Mark McMillan. Younger children might enjoy Doug Horley's *Woopah Wahey* or John Hardwick's *For God So Loved the World.*

- **Write a journal entry** or letter of thanks to Jesus. Nobody else has to read it.

- **Create an acrostic poem** by trying to think of different things you are grateful for, beginning with every letter of the words THANK YOU.

- **Spend some quiet time** looking at a cross, or a picture of the crucifixion that speaks to you.

- **Read the story** of the crucifixion, either from a Bible or from a children's version. Stop every now and then to simply say 'Thank you' out loud.

DAY 7

Remind yourselves of this week's story by looking back at the reading and retelling from Day 1. The Bible doesn't tell us any more about the rich young ruler: what do you think happened next? Have a go at writing a story or sketch, or improvise with some small world play figures standing in for the characters, to imagine what the rich young ruler did next. Alternatively, you could try writing a letter to him and giving him your advice. What would you do if you were him?

Zacchaeus

Introduction

Zacchaeus is a fun story, made familiar by Sunday school songs such as 'Zacchaeus was a wee little man'. It has always been a popular one to tell children, perhaps because of that simple detail that Zacchaeus was short – most children can relate to being unable to see over the heads of a crowd. The most important part of the story, however, is the way in which Zacchaeus was able to change his life after being called and accepted by Jesus. He went from selfishness to generosity in the space of one meal, and is an example of what repentance looks like: not a grudging, law-based, fearful change, but a total redirection of life, fuelled by joy and filled with hope.

DAY 1

Telling

> He entered Jericho and was passing through it. A man was there named Zacchaeus; he was a chief tax-collector and was rich. He was trying to see who Jesus was, but on account of the crowd he could not, because he was short in stature. So he ran ahead and climbed a sycamore tree to see him, because he was going to pass that way. When Jesus came to the place, he looked up and said to him, 'Zacchaeus, hurry and come down; for I must stay at your house today.' So he hurried down and was happy to welcome him. All who saw it began to grumble and said, 'He has gone to be the guest of one who is a sinner.' Zacchaeus stood there and said to

the Lord, 'Look, half of my possessions, Lord, I will give to the poor; and if I have defrauded anyone of anything, I will pay back four times as much.' Then Jesus said to him, 'Today salvation has come to this house, because he too is a son of Abraham.'

Luke 19:1-9

Retelling

Tips and ideas for telling this story:

This is a fun, fast telling with a growing rhyme. Each short rhyming word or phrase has an action, and the rhymes are collected and repeated as you go through the telling until you have a short action rhyme with which to remember the story later. As often as possible, use a silly voice for the rhyming phrases as well as an action, to make them really memorable, and always use the same intonation when you say them: 'Tiny wee!' in a squeaky voice, for example, or 'Home for tea' in a sing-song. Each time the rhymes are listed, add to the hilarity by getting faster!

As well as the rhymes, ask your listeners to make a thumbs-down action and say 'boo!' whenever they hear the words 'tax collector', and to turn up their noses and say 'hmph!' whenever they hear the word 'Pharisee'. We've met tax collectors and Pharisees before, in Week Two, but this is a quick and easy way to remember the general opinion of these groups without interrupting the story with extra explanations.

Once, there was a man called Zacchaeus, and Zacchaeus was a tax collector (booo!). Because he was a tax collector (booo!), nobody liked him. He was also a very short person. In fact, Zacchaeus was tiny wee! Can you say 'tiny wee' and hold up your fingers to show how little he was?

One day, Zacchaeus heard that Jesus would be walking nearby. Zacchaeus was very curious to see what Jesus was like, as he'd heard a lot about him. But when he went out to see, he found that there were crowds already lining the road, and because he was so short, he couldn't see. Can you say 'couldn't see' and cover your eyes?

So Zacchaeus was tiny wee, and couldn't see . . .

He looked around and saw that there was a sycamore tree beside the road, so he climbed up into its branches to get a better view. Can you say 'climbed a tree' and do a climbing action?

Zacchaeus was tiny wee; couldn't see; climbed a tree . . .

And from the top of the tree, Zacchaeus could see everyone in the crowd, even all the Pharisees (hmph!). They were all looking at the road, and along the road came Jesus. Everybody crowded him, hoping that he would talk to them, heal them or even just smile at them. They were all saying, 'Pick me, pick me!' Can you say that, and wave your hand in the air?

Zacchaeus was tiny wee; couldn't see; climbed a tree; pick me, pick me!

But Jesus kept walking until he got to the bottom of Zacchaeus' tree. Then he stopped, and looked up – straight at Zacchaeus. 'Come on down, Zacchaeus!' he said. 'Will you take me home for tea?' Can you say, 'home for tea' and pretend to drink from a tea cup? – pinkies in the air!

Zacchaeus was tiny wee; couldn't see; climbed a tree; pick me, pick me; home for tea . . .

So Zacchaeus got down from his tree and took Jesus to his house. Can you guess who wasn't very happy about that? The Pharisees! (hmph!). They said, 'This man is a tax collector (boooo!) and Jesus shouldn't hang around with people like that!'

But Zacchaeus said to Jesus, 'I haven't led a good life – and I'm really sorry.' Can you put on your sorriest face and say 'sor-ryyy!'?

Zacchaeus was tiny wee; couldn't see; climbed a tree; pick me, pick me; home for tea; sor-ryyyy!

Zacchaeus said, 'In fact, I'm so sorry that, right now, I'm going to give half my money to the poor; and to all the people I've cheated and stolen from, I'm going to pay back four times as much.' Then everybody saw that Zacchaeus was a changed man – can you punch the air and yell 'Yippee!'?

So now, do you remember the story? Zacchaeus was . . . tiny wee; couldn't see; climbed a tree; pick me, pick me; home for tea; sor-ryyyy; YIPPEE!

DAY 2

Craft

Helicopter seed

Sycamore trees have seeds that act like little helicopters, spinning as they float to the ground. Have you ever made a paper sycamore seed flyer? It's very easy. All you need is a sheet of paper, a pair of scissors and a paper clip.

Begin by folding your paper in half, bringing the two longest sides together, then unfolding again so that you can see the crease.

Next, fold the top third of the paper down, make a crease and unfold it again.

Now, use the scissors to cut down the middle fold of your paper, from the top, stopping at the crease a third of the way down.

Fold the paper along the middle crease again, and look at the bottom two thirds. You are going to cut a tall rectangle off the corner, so that when you unfold the paper, you have a T shape at the bottom.

Finally, weight the bottom of the T with the paper clip and fold down the two flaps that you made at the top, one towards the front and the other towards the back: these are your helicopter blade.

When you drop your 'seed' from a height, it should spin as it falls to the ground.

Keep your paper seed for Day 7's prayer activity this week.

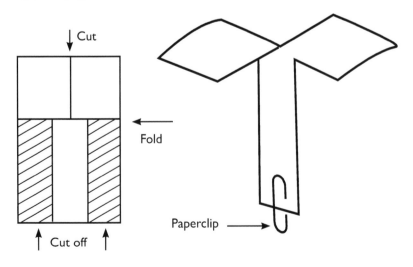

Story card

Make a moving card to help you tell the story of Zacchaeus. You'll need some card, some green paper, glue or sticky tape, and scissors.

Draw a tree with bare branches on the left of your card. Draw (or cut from a magazine and stick on) a figure to be Jesus under the tree on the right. On a separate piece of card, draw (or cut from a magazine) a little figure to be Zacchaeus, and cut him out.

Cut a strip of card about 2cm wide and 10cm long, and stick Zacchaeus to the bottom of it.

Next, cut out a cloud shape from green card or paper: this will be the leaves for your tree. Stick the shape over the branches by putting glue only on the left and right sides, leaving a space through the middle to slot in your strip of card. Now you should be able to push the card to lower Zacchaeus down from the tree, or pull it to hide him under the leaves again.

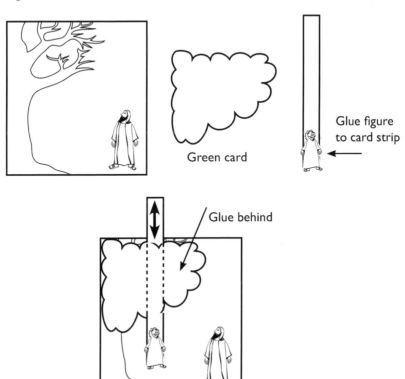

Green card

Glue figure to card strip

Glue behind

DAY 3

Context

Today holds an opportunity to look back over the stories and people that we have encountered so far since the beginning of Lent.

The story of Zacchaeus has lots of similarities with that of Levi: they are both tax collectors, they both host a meal for Jesus and, both times, the Pharisees complain. However, their reactions to Jesus' call are different. While Levi leaves everything behind to follow Jesus, becoming an evangelist in the process, Zacchaeus divides up his money to make amends and leads a changed life where he is. His joyful release of his possessions contrasts with the rich young ruler, who couldn't manage to let go of his riches.

Each of the characters have had different approaches to Jesus as well. The fishermen were fearful when they saw what Jesus could do, and Simon even asked Jesus to go away at first; whereas the rich young ruler was bold enough to walk up and ask a question. Zacchaeus was curious, too, but only from the safe distance of his tree; and Levi, as far as we know, was simply minding his own business before the direct simplicity of Jesus' call swept him off his feet.

Thinking about all these stories, and about your own experiences of Jesus, which character do you think you are most like?

DAY 4

Act

Zacchaeus reacted to the grace and acceptance of Jesus with what Christians would call an act of repentance. The word 'repent' is not just another word for 'apologise', but also carries a sense of a change, of a U-turn in behaviour or lifestyle. Zacchaeus didn't just say sorry, he set about making right the things he had done wrong. Today's act is both very simple and very difficult. Can you think of anybody who needs an apology from you? It may be someone in the recent past, or a relationship that was broken long ago. If you feel you can, take the first step towards a reconciliation today. It may take the form of a conversation, phone call, letter or adding somebody as a friend on social media. It may be that someone in your own family needs the apology.

If you can't think of an example in your life at the moment, then look out for situations today where you could try to be the peacemaker, and, as Jesus did for Zacchaeus, encourage a friend to do an about-turn and say sorry. If you don't feel you can step in directly, then pray for peace in any situation that you see. And if none of this seems to apply to you today, then have a look at tomorrow's task . . .

DAY 5

Community Day

When Zacchaeus made amends, he did so in a generous-hearted way, giving back even more than he had taken and giving away extra as well. He changed his whole lifestyle to help people who had been harmed by the way he lived before.

We don't like to think that our lifestyles might be doing harm to others, but the evidence says that the way we live and spend our money can have a huge effect on our community, from our rubbish destroying the environment to our clothing and food choices contributing to exploitation and slavery.

Today's challenge is to find one way to change your family's lifestyle, not just today, but from now on. It might be deciding to start recycling; agreeing to stop buying one particular product with packaging that goes to landfill; switching to a more sustainable alternative for something you use often; doing a litter pick on the way home from school every day; or boycotting chocolate that doesn't have a slavery-free certification.

Those are only a few suggestions! Spend some time together today, researching and talking about what you might do. Why not ask others in your church and community what they think? They may be able to help out with ideas of local projects or resources.

DAY 6

Retelling

Tips and ideas for telling this story:
Here is the story of Zacchaeus written for you to tell with your story card craft from Day 2 of this week. Slide the little Zacchaeus up and down to go with the words in **bold**. You could also tell it by bending your knees and crouching down to the ground for every 'down', and stretching up tall for every 'up'. You could use this as a game, repeating it several times and getting faster each time until somebody goes the wrong way or misses one. It's quite a work-out!

Zacchaeus was feeling low. Nothing could cheer him **up**. Nobody liked him, and he felt really **down**! When Jesus came to town, Zacchaeus thought he'd go and look him **up**. But when he got there, he was too far **down** to see! So Zacchaeus climbed **up** a tall tree. From the top of the tree he could see **down** to the crowd, and there was Jesus looking **up**! 'Zacchaeus, come **down**!' called Jesus, 'I'm going to your house today!' Zacchaeus was so excited he didn't know which way was **up**! He quickly climbed **down** from the tree and went with Jesus. The Pharisees were fed **up**, but Zacchaeus told them to calm **down**. 'I'm giving **up** my old ways,' he said, 'and I'm going to pay back everyone that I've let **down**.'

DAY 7

Prayer

Use your helicopter seed craft from Day 2 for this prayer activity, which is all about reconciliation and letting go.

On Day 4, we thought of people who might need our apologies, but the other side to reconciliation is forgiveness. It can be very hard to forgive when somebody has hurt us, but Jesus says that it's important to forgive others in order to receive God's forgiveness. Zacchaeus was able to let go of his ill-gotten gains when he received forgiveness and acceptance from Jesus. Can we let go of past hurts and grudges when we receive peace and forgiveness?

Find a high place – the top of the stairs, a balcony, a climbing frame, or perhaps even a tree like Zacchaeus! On your helicopter seed, write the initials of someone you'd like to forgive, or draw another sign or symbol to represent the situation you are thinking of. Ask God to help you to stop bearing a grudge against that person, and say a prayer for them to find peace. Then let go of your paper seed and watch it spiral to the ground.

Take up Your Cross

Introduction

This final week of Lent looks at some of the more difficult sayings of Jesus as he talks about his own death and explains what it will mean to follow him. This is serious stuff, but in the light of the stories we've heard and the characters we've met over the last five weeks, we gain a better understanding of the sacrifices involved and, more importantly, of the reasons for making them.

DAY 1

Telling

> Then he said to them all, 'If any want to become my followers, let them deny themselves and take up their cross daily and follow me. For those who want to save their life will lose it, and those who lose their life for my sake will save it. What does it profit them if they gain the whole world, but lose or forfeit themselves? Those who are ashamed of me and of my words, of them the Son of Man will be ashamed when he comes in his glory and the glory of the Father and of the holy angels. But truly I tell you, there are some standing here who will not taste death before they see the kingdom of God.'
>
> *Luke 9:23-27*

Here we have a clear instruction from Jesus about how to follow him. 'Deny yourself, take up your cross daily and follow me.' What does he mean? How can we follow this instruction?

Doubtless some of those listening would later take up literal crosses and follow Jesus by dying as martyrs. But Jesus says to take up a cross 'daily'. He is talking about a kind of death that can happen over and over again.

Today, the phrase 'carry your cross' has been used to mean 'put up with troubling things'. For example, 'The bus doesn't stop in my village, and that's our cross to bear!' I don't think that Jesus is talking here about the troubles and concerns, whether trivial or serious, that people put up with every day.

When Jesus talks about taking up a cross, he may be meaning something similar to the cost of following him that we explored in Week Three: the things that we need to give up, or let go, in order to live our lives to the full. The cross we have to carry is the one on which we daily put to death the person we would be without Jesus, and the way we would be living if we had never encountered him.

Over the past weeks, we have met people whose lives were changed when they heard Jesus say 'Follow me.' If the fishermen from our first story had never encountered Jesus, they would have remained in their self-sufficient, predictable routine of daily fishing, but their reliance on those things died when they started to follow him. They took up a cross of uncertainty and risk. Levi and Zacchaeus, too, took up crosses of poverty and humility so that the greedy part of them would die. The rich young ruler found the cross of poverty too heavy to carry.

As Christians looking back after the first Easter, we know that Jesus has paid the price for our failure to live as his people, and in response we take up our own cross and follow him. Jesus helps us to carry our crosses, as every day we receive forgiveness from him. We put our old selves to death and live new lives as people who have been changed by Jesus.

Today, make a small cross using whatever you can find – twigs, paper, card – or perhaps you can find one from a necklace. Keep it in your pocket as a reminder of Jesus' request that we choose to follow him daily, and of everything he did to help us do that. Why not make one as a gift for somebody else as well?

DAY 2

Telling

> When the days drew near for him to be taken up, he set his face to go to Jerusalem . . .

> As they were going along the road, someone said to him, 'I will follow you wherever you go.' And Jesus said to him, 'Foxes have holes, and birds of the air have nests; but the Son of Man has nowhere to lay his head.' To another he said, 'Follow me.' But he said, 'Lord, first let me go and bury my father.' But Jesus said to him, 'Let the dead bury their own dead; but as for you, go and proclaim the kingdom of God.' Another said, 'I will follow you, Lord; but let me first say farewell to those at my home.' Jesus said to him, 'No one who puts a hand to the plough and looks back is fit for the kingdom of God.'

Luke 9:51, 57-62

Retelling

Tips and ideas for telling this story:

There is a sense of urgency in this passage because, as verse 51 tells us, Jesus has already 'set his face to go to Jerusalem'. In other words, even this early in the Gospel, he is determinedly heading for the cross. When he tells his would-be followers that they can't plough a straight line if they look behind them, he is already putting his own advice into practice. What excuses and barriers to following Jesus do we have today? Are they anything like the ones he answers in this passage?

This song-poem doesn't have a tune, but can be very effective performed in several voices: say the chorus (in **bold**) rhythmically all together, then have two voices for each verse, one to read the first four lines and the other to read the lines in italics.

Once you've set the destination on your sat nav,
it's no good turning round and looking back.
Once you're on the road, the whole adventure's started –
never mind about the things you didn't pack.
Once you're certain of the reason for your journey,
once you're headed to the place you long to see,
once you've set the destination on your sat nav –
you can't go back to where you used to be.

I think I'd like to join the journey, Jesus,
but – will there be a pretty place to stay?
Somewhere nice and quiet in the country
or a smart hotel for us to get away?
The foxes and the birds may have their hideouts:
for us, there isn't any guarantee.
We might end up in slums or with the homeless –
but if we do, will you still come with me?

Once you've set the destination on your sat nav…

I think I'd like to join the journey, Jesus,
but people here might think the worst of me,
and anyway, my family still needs me.
Perhaps I'll wait until I'm really free.
The people that we care for may not follow.
They might see what we do and disagree.
We'll have to let them make their own decisions –
but if they do, will you still come with me?

Once you've set the destination on your sat nav…

I think I'd like to join the journey, Jesus,
but I might miss the things I leave behind,

the things I used to do and have and live for –
will there be better things for me to find?
We'll have to hold our loved possessions loosely
while heaven's treasures can be hard to see,
but once you've started ploughing this new furrow,
you can't look back to who you used to be.

Once you've set the destination on your sat nav...

DAY 3

Context

Jesus did not just tell us to give things up and resist temptations. He led the way by doing it himself. Today, use areas in your own home to walk through the story of Jesus' temptation in the wilderness. (You will find the story in your Bible in Luke 4:1-13.)

First area: a place with running water, like a bathroom. Run a basin of water and let everybody splash their hands in it. Explain that this story takes place just after Jesus was baptised in the river Jordan. He knew that he was about to start three difficult and demanding years of travelling, teaching and ministry. He knew that he needed to prepare himself, and so he went into the wilderness.

Second area: outside your front door, if you can stand there safely, or gathered in the doorway. Explain that Jesus left behind any comforts, places and people that he knew and went to a place outside where there was nothing. He gave up food and drink and stayed there for 40 days.

Third area: the place where food is prepared. Explain that after 40 days, the devil came to tempt Jesus, knowing that all would be lost if only Jesus would do something outside of God's will. The first thing the devil tried was to get Jesus to use his divine power to satisfy the needs of his body. After 40 days, Jesus was starving, so the devil suggested that he turned stones into bread. But Jesus said, 'It is written that people shall not live by bread alone, but by the words of God.'

Fourth area: any window, preferably the one with the furthest view. Explain that the second thing the devil tried was to get Jesus to give up his heavenly power to gain earthly power. He took him to a high place and showed him a view of the world, saying that it would all be his, if only he would worship the devil instead of God. Jesus replied with another piece of scripture: 'It is written, "Worship the Lord your God, and serve only him."'

Fifth area: the highest place in your home, whether that means top floor, roof or balancing on the dining table! Explain that the devil then tried to persuade Jesus to test out his divinity by jumping from the roof of the temple. The devil also used quotations from scripture himself, saying that angels would protect Jesus. But Jesus replied: 'It is also written, "Do not put God to the test."'

Sixth area: a comfortable place such as a sofa or bed. Explain that after these three temptations, the devil left Jesus, and angels arrived to look after him and make him comfortable. Now that he was ready to begin his ministry, he left the wilderness again.

DAY 4

Community Day

We have seen that the first disciples gave up a predictable, routine lifestyle and took on risk and randomness when they followed Jesus. What could you do today that would take you one step out of your comfort zone?

Could you say hello to a Big Issue seller and buy a copy of the magazine? Could you offer a homeless person a sandwich? Could you strike up a conversation with a stranger waiting in the same queue? Could you offer to pray for someone? Could you pay for a stranger's shopping? Keep an eye and an ear out today for an opportunity to do something random, uncomfortable and generous! You never know where God will want to send you.

DAY 5

Palm Sunday

Today is Palm Sunday, when the Church remembers Jesus' triumphant entry into Jerusalem, riding on a donkey and cheered by crowds – crowds that less than a week later were calling for him to be crucified.

Find a church today where you can join in and celebrate the king who comes riding on a donkey. A service with a procession is even better!

Here is a song that goes to the tune of an old sea shanty called 'Donkey Riding' and tells the story of Palm Sunday. You might like to use it today.

Jesus, with his group of friends
going to Jerusalem
called them near and said to them,
'Go and find a donkey!'

Hey ho and away we go
donkey riding, donkey riding.
Hey ho and away we go
riding on a donkey!

Two disciples went ahead
a donkey's colt away they led,
when the owner asked, they said
'The master needs your donkey!'

Hey ho . . .

So they brought the donkey back,
spread their coats upon its back,
and some more along the track
where Jesus rode the donkey.

Hey ho . . .

Crowds and crowds were gathering,
and they all began to sing
loud hosannas to the king
who rides upon a donkey.

Hey ho . . .

DAY 6

Prayer

Dear Jesus, following you is an adventure! You promise us life to the full, but only when we are prepared to give up our own plans for our lives and let you go first. We know that we could be asked to do things that are difficult, sacrifice things that are precious and resist things that are inviting. Thank you that you did all of that, and more, for us. Let us do the same for you. Make us ready for anything!

DAY 7

Wondering into Holy Week

As we prepare to join Jesus in his last few days before his crucifixion and resurrection, take some time to look back over all the people and places we have encountered since the beginning of Lent, and 'go wondering' together by discussing these questions. You don't have to use all the questions: talk about what interests you and is most relevant to your family.

- Which stories and characters do you remember? Which were your favourites?
- Did you identify with any character in particular? If so, why?
- What did you most enjoy doing together as a family?
- Did you do anything that you think you will try again more regularly?

- Have you seen any results, in your family and the community around you, from following this guide?

- Can you think of anything you have learned over the last six weeks that you didn't know before?

- If you could go back in time now, and be in Jerusalem to see the events of the coming week, who and where would you like to be – a disciple, one of Jesus' close friends, a member of the crowd, a soldier, an animal? Why not try to imagine and write down your experiences as that character over the coming week?

Holy Week

Introduction

The liturgical season of Lent officially ends on Maundy Thursday, even though people who have given something up for Lent won't take it up again before Easter Sunday. The focus now shifts from preparation to experience. Here are some suggestions to take your family through the moving, real-time experience of Holy Week.

Maundy Thursday

On Maundy Thursday, Christians remember the events that took place at the Last Supper, when Jesus gave his disciples bread and wine which he referred to as his body and his blood. The three synoptic Gospels (Matthew, Mark and Luke) all mention this special meal: you can find it in Luke 22:7-39. The Gospel of John, while it does not mention the sharing of bread and wine, includes much more detail about the conversation at the table and the last teachings of Jesus, as well as the moment in which Jesus takes a towel and a bowl and washes his disciples' feet, modelling the way that they should serve one another. You can read John's account in chapters 13-17.

Today, find a version or versions of the story that you like, and read and remember together. You could try washing each other's feet, or you could have a special meal and pass bread and wine to each other afterwards. You could also remember Jesus' repeated instructions to love and serve one another by each person choosing one thing that the other members of the family could do for them, and then doing all of them, making sure that nobody is left out of either serving or being served.

At the end of the meal, Jesus went out into the garden to pray: later, he was arrested there. Some churches hold a 'watch' or vigil of silent prayer, remembering that Jesus asked his disciples to wait and pray with him, but they were too tired and fell asleep. At the end of the day, try to spend some time in prayer or silence with each other.

Good Friday

It is not easy to explain the events of Good Friday to children. The crucifixion involves more violence than we would be happy for our children to see on a screen or read about in a book. As well as that, children all have very different experiences and understandings of death and what it means to die. It is natural to want to protect our children from a subject that might distress them, especially if they are so little that it doesn't seem necessary to talk about such things yet.

On the other hand, Jesus told us to become like little children to enter the kingdom of God. If he requires a child-like understanding from us, perhaps we can be the ones to learn from our children's reactions to the story of Good Friday. It is a sad story: part of the purpose of the way the Church remembers the story in real time is so that we can remember that it was terrible, and experience some of that sadness. Without it, the Easter joy is less joyful. The same goes for children, and perhaps we should not be nervous about allowing them to feel sad.

Having said all of that, there is no need to show children the goriest parts of Jesus' death on the cross. The story is full of little stories: others' experiences as they observed the events. If we are worried about our children looking too closely at the cross, we can tell the story at one remove: from the point of view of a disciple who ran away and was told about it later by the others, or Pontius Pilate's wife who warned him not to get involved, or Barabbas, the thief freed instead of Jesus, who was probably the first person to realise that Jesus had died in his place.

These perspectives offer many different experiences of the crucifixion and its meaning for us as Christians. In particular, there are all the people who received comfort or forgiveness from Jesus, even while he was in agony and dying. Here, as just one example, is a mother's story:

> My son is dead, a death by cruelty:
> fixed to a cross and left alone to die.
> Perhaps his crimes deserved that death, though why
> I cannot see.
>
> I watched them – from the crowd I saw him die.
> Although they pressed his hands against the beam
> the wind blew out the anguish in his scream.
> I could not cry.
>
> Another man was hanging there as well.
> I fancied he turned just before the end
> and spoke to my dear son, as would a friend.
> I could not tell.
>
> But others told me, who could hear his voice,
> that it is true: the stranger spoke to say
> my son would be with him that very day
> in Paradise.
>
> My boy, they tell me, seemed to find relief
> in those brave words: and so I too am glad
> this man, though dying, comforted my lad,
> a common thief.

Holy Saturday

Holy Saturday is a strange, quiet day: a space to remember that Jesus really did die, and that his friends and followers didn't know the end of the story.

Try making an Easter garden today. Place soil, moss, grass, and flowers into a seed tray. A flowerpot on its side and a large, flat stone make a tomb; or you could build one with a pile of stones, or make one out of clay. Today, the tomb is sealed shut – but make sure that you will be able to roll the stone to one side tomorrow morning!

Easter Sunday
Telling

> After these things Jesus showed himself again to the disciples by the Sea of Tiberias; and he showed himself in this way. Gathered there together were Simon Peter, Thomas called the Twin, Nathanael of Cana in Galilee, the sons of Zebedee, and two others of his disciples. Simon Peter said to them, 'I am going fishing.' They said to him, 'We will go with you.' They went out and got into the boat, but that night they caught nothing.
>
> Just after daybreak, Jesus stood on the beach; but the disciples did not know that it was Jesus. Jesus said to them, 'Children, you have no fish, have you?' They answered him, 'No.' He said to them, 'Cast the net to the right side of the boat, and you will find some.' So they cast it, and now they were not able to haul it in because there were so many fish. That disciple whom Jesus loved said to Peter, 'It is the Lord!' When Simon Peter heard that it was the Lord, he put on some clothes, for he was naked, and jumped into the lake. But the other disciples came in the boat, dragging the net full of fish, for they were not far from the land, only about a hundred yards off.
>
> When they had gone ashore, they saw a charcoal fire there, with fish on it, and bread. Jesus said to them, 'Bring some of the fish that you have just caught.' So Simon Peter went aboard and hauled

the net ashore, full of large fish, a hundred and fifty-three of them; and though there were so many, the net was not torn. Jesus said to them, 'Come and have breakfast.' Now none of the disciples dared to ask him, 'Who are you?' because they knew it was the Lord. Jesus came and took the bread and gave it to them, and did the same with the fish. This was now the third time that Jesus appeared to the disciples after he was raised from the dead.

When they had finished breakfast, Jesus said to Simon Peter, 'Simon son of John, do you love me more than these?' He said to him, 'Yes, Lord; you know that I love you.' Jesus said to him, 'Feed my lambs.' A second time he said to him, 'Simon son of John, do you love me?' He said to him, 'Yes, Lord; you know that I love you.' Jesus said to him, 'Tend my sheep.' He said to him the third time, 'Simon son of John, do you love me?' Peter felt hurt because he said to him the third time, 'Do you love me?' And he said to him, 'Lord, you know everything; you know that I love you.' Jesus said to him, 'Feed my sheep. Very truly, I tell you, when you were younger, you used to fasten your own belt and to go wherever you wished. But when you grow old, you will stretch out your hands, and someone else will fasten a belt around you and take you where you do not wish to go.' (He said this to indicate the kind of death by which he would glorify God.) After this he said to him, 'Follow me.'

John 21:1-19

Retelling

Tips and ideas for telling this story:

Here is Simon Peter, the fisherman from our very first story, to tell the story of one of Jesus' resurrection appearances: the one that meant the most to him. A first person telling is ideal for explaining plenty of background without having to put long asides into the story: if you tell it out loud, remain in character as Peter throughout. Woven together with the rest of Peter's story, this version provides some ideas about how and why this appearance was so significant, both for Simon Peter and for us today.

I could never get a thing right, you know. I mean, none of us could, but I was probably the worst of the twelve when it came to putting my foot right in it. I didn't have a clue what was going on, half the time. I seemed to get most things wrong when I was only trying to be helpful. Stop the children from disturbing Jesus? No, apparently they're the most important people in the kingdom of heaven. Stop Jesus from going into Jerusalem to get killed? Wrong again. I got called Satan that time. Suggest that the Messiah shouldn't be washing my dirty feet? Wrong! Interrupt a transcendent experience on top of a mountain by offering to put up some tents? Typical me. Typical silly old Simon Peter.

Never thought I'd get it quite as wrong as I did in the end. Never thought I'd pretend I didn't know him. I always imagined I'd be the one there for him when he really needed me. But I wasn't. He died, and I'm sure he knew that I had denied knowing him three times, just like he said I would.

So when the tomb was empty, and the women were rushing around saying they'd seen him and talking about angels, and he started appearing in locked rooms and showing everyone the holes in his hands where the nails had been, it was hard to explain why I was the only one not jumping for joy. I think I didn't feel part of it any more. I'd already failed, you see. Didn't think I was going to get to do . . . well, whatever it was they were all about to do.

So I took James and John and a few of the other guys, and we went fishing. Only thing I know I can do without making mistakes. Except I obviously can't, because by morning we still hadn't caught a thing.

Then there was a shout from the beach: 'You haven't caught anything, have you?' I thought someone else had got up early just to make fun of us.

'Not a thing,' I called back.

'Try putting the net on the other side of the boat,' this stranger shouted.

With a strange sense of déjà vu, we hauled the net over the other side of the boat, and immediately it was wriggling with fish.

'This has happened before,' I said to John, as we struggled together to contain the fish. He gave me a funny look. 'Of course it has!' he said.

It took me that long to work out that it was Jesus standing on the beach, filling our nets with fish exactly the way he had done when we first followed him. After that I didn't waste any time. I left the boat and the fish, jumped straight into the water and started to swim.

I crawled out of the sea at his feet, soaking and sandy, still trying to work out a way to tell him how sorry I was, but he spoke first. Giving me a hand to stand up, he grinned, 'Haven't you brought any of those fish? I've got a fire going ready for breakfast!'

The other guys came in with the boat and we did have breakfast after that. Jesus roasted the fish on the fire. John insisted on counting them all first. If there are any fishermen reading this who are interested in knowing what the catch of a lifetime looks like, there were exactly one hundred and fifty-three fish.

Jesus and I went for a walk along the shore. I wanted so much to ask him whether he was here for good now, whether things were going to go back to normal, whether he knew what I'd done and how sorry I was, but this time I kept my mouth shut. I wasn't going to risk spoiling the fragile moment by getting it wrong again. Eventually, he spoke.

'Simon son of John, do you love me?'

I thought it must be all over then. He hadn't used the name he gave me – Peter – and he needed to ask whether I, of all people, loved him?

'You know that I do,' I mumbled.

'Feed my lambs,' he said, and then he repeated the first question: 'Simon son of John, do you love me?'

'Yes, Lord, you know I do!'

'Look after my sheep. Simon son of John, do you love me?'

I couldn't stand it. 'Lord, you know everything, don't you?' I asked, daring to look into his face. Yes, he knew. Three times I'd denied having anything to do with him. Was he giving me three chances to explain myself? 'You know that I love you,' I whispered.

'Feed my sheep. You know, there were times when you could get up and go wherever you wanted. But when you grow old, you will hold out your hands and somebody else will lead you into places you don't want to go.'

I was beginning to understand: and the next thing he said confirmed it. This was my second chance, you see. That's why he had come to the beach where I first left everything for him, and performed the same sign with all the fish that had first convinced me he was Lord. That's why he had asked me three times whether I loved him and why he had used my old name. It wasn't a punishment after all: he had already forgiven me for what I had done. He was putting the choice back into my hands: whether to go back to my old life and be Simon, son of John, the fisherman, or whether to carry on with him as Peter, fisher of men. It was all summed up in the next two words he said.

'Follow me.'

FOLLOW ME!

FOLLOW ME!

Daily Lent Guide for Families

AMY ROBINSON

kevin
mayhew